Using ChatGPT technology for marketing

Index

The command prompt is a powerful tool that can help marketing professionals automate tasks, analyze data, and improve the efficiency of their work. In this book, we present how to use command prompt for marketing, using ChatGPT technology.

For example, we show practical ways to use command prompt for data analysis, creating custom scripts, managing marketing campaigns, and other important tasks for marketing professionals. You will learn how to integrate command prompt with other digital marketing tools and use ChatGPT to maximize productivity and accuracy in your work.

By the end of the book, you will have a solid understanding of how to use command prompt for marketing and how ChatGPT technology can be useful in this process. This book is essential reading for any marketing professional who wants to improve their efficiency and accuracy in their work.

Blogging

Comands:

Write a Blog outline for an article about [TOPIC]

The outline should be a list of 10 headings

Write a 2 paragraph blog introduction for an article about [TOPIC]. The introduction should be a maximum of 200 words. Make it highly engaging and hook the reader in.

Write a short and sweet blog conclusion for an article about [TOPIC]. The conclusion should be a maximum of 200 words. Briefly summarize the article with a list of 5 bullet points. Make it concise.

Add a call to action for [product/service]

"Write a completely unique 2000 word article about ""TOPIC""

OPTIONAL PRODUCT/SERVICE DETAILS] - e.g. AtOnce is an AI writing, AI customer service tool… works with Shopify, Woocommerce… etc.

[DESCRIPTION OF FORMATTING] - e.g. add <p> </p> tags, add bullet points etc

[OUTLINE TO USE] Make it highly engaging. Write for the level of a 5th grader. Make it unique. Do not repeat yourself. [Insert any extra details here]

[EXTRA INFORMATION TO INCLUDE] - e.g. add counterarguments to topic. Address common reader concerns around the topic. Write a list of 10 frequently asked questions

Finish off the article in the same format. Make it highly engaging.

"Extending articles: Write [X] highly engaging, detailed paragraphs in the same format. Include bullet points. Do not include the same points as above. Write new points. Make it engaging."

Business

Commands:

Can you predict new company concepts without funding?

Send an email requesting that people act more quickly.

Please use the following job description and my resume to write a letter

Please share the meeting's agenda in advance.

Please create a product roadmap for Instagram's storie in order to increase the number of posts. Please be as detailed as possible, and whenever possible, use comparisons to other tools such as TikTok.

Let's brainstorm business ideas together on meal delivery service. You will ask yourself 1000 questions that should generate more ideas and you will answer to these questions.

Write a 50 words copy for a product called "BizGrowth" that helps struggling content creators get more followers and earn money in 30 days with guarantee, then ask them to sign up at BizGrowth.io

Generate digital startup ideas based on the wish of the people. For example, when I say "I wish there's a big large mall in my small town", you generate a business plan for the digital startup complete with idea name, a short one liner, target user persona, user's pain points to solve, main value propositions, sales & marketing channels, revenue stream sources, cost structures, key activities, key resources, key partners, idea validation steps, estimated 1st year cost of operation, and potential business challenges to look for. Write the result in a markdown table.

Creat a list of 21 objections a customer might have about the new, healthy soda made with plant fiber and prebiotics, called Olipop

Write a first-person account from a character named Rob of what it feels like to be copywriter struggling with getting clients from Upwork. Be very specific about the problems Rob faces and what he feels like day to day.

Act as a headline generator and provide 15 headlines based on the following keywords: kombucha, organic, billions of probiotics, alcoholic drink, fun

Create a 50 day return policy for my e-commerce website outlining that the customer does have send the product by requesting a return shipping label for refunds and exchanges. Make the tone upbeat, positive and inspiring.

Outline a 10-point sales page promoting a teeth whitening serum endorsed by dozens of celebrities and renown dentists to get millenial women to try the first shipment of the product for free. Make the copy funny, friendly and easy to read.

Give me 10 ideas for attention-grabbing hooks I can do during the first 3 seconds of a TikTok video on the 10 best cities to visit in the United States if you like to eat donuts. The goal is to stop someone from scrolling and watching the video.

Write a contract for my Ecommerce client paying my company $3000 per month with the invoice due net 30

Write a GDPR-compliant privacy policy for my website about natural candles outlining how the site will handle intellectual property and personal data

Write a job posting for [job role] requiring [experience] and performing these key tasks [list of tasks]

Copywriting

Comands:

Rewrite a piece of copy to make it more concise.

Write a headline that grabs attention and draws readers in.

Create a copywriting template to use for common pieces.

Brainstorm ways to make a piece of copy more engaging.

Come up with 3 different titles for a piece of writing.

Analyze the effectiveness of a piece of copy and make improvements.

Write a piece of copy from the perspective of a customer.

Develop a persuasive argument for a product or service.

Rewrite a piece of copy to make it more persuasive.

Analyze the grammar and punctuation in a piece of copy.

Research the target audience for a piece of copy.

Try to write a piece of copy in two different styles.

Write a piece of copy that is easy to read and understand.

Rewrite a piece of copy to make it more accessible.

Develop a style guide for a specific type of copy and establish consistency among them.

Find 5 pieces of copy that you admire and analyze what makes them successful.

Rewrite a piece of copy to make it more suitable for a different audience.

Brainstorm ideas for a new series of blog posts on a particular topic.

Rewrite a piece of copy to make it more SEO-friendly.

Analyze the structure of a piece of copy and make improvements.

Research the competition and write a comparison between them and your product.

Write a piece of copy that addresses a common customer objection.

Rewrite a piece of copy to make it more conversational.

Develop an elevator pitch for a new product or service.

Rewrite a piece of copy to make it more personal and relatable.

Write a case study that highlights the success of a customer.

Brainstorm ideas for a series of emails to engage customers.

Write a piece of copy that is targeted for a specific demographic.

Develop a voice and tone guide for a specific type of copy.

Analyze a piece of copy and identify the techniques used to make the writing persuasive.

Rewrite a piece of copy to make it more memorable.

Brainstorm ideas for a new whitepaper on a particular topic.

Rewrite a piece of copy to make it more appealing to a younger demographic.

Analyze the tone of a piece of copy and make improvements.

Research the target audience for a piece of copy and develop a profile.

Write a piece of copy that promotes the benefits of a product.

Rewrite a piece of copy to make it more accurate and factual.

Develop a call-to-action that encourages readers to take action.

Rewrite a piece of copy to make it more engaging and entertaining.

Write a case study that highlights the success of a customer's experience.

Brainstorm ideas for a series of social media posts on a particular topic.

Write a piece of copy that is targeted for a specific region or country.

Develop a style guide for a specific type of copy and establish consistency.

Rewrite a piece of copy to make it more convincing.

Write a headline that stands out and catches readers' attention.

Develop a template for writing persuasive copy.

Brainstorm ways to make a piece of copy more concise.

Rewrite a piece of copy to make it more informative.

Research the target audience for a piece of copy and write for them.

Write a piece of copy that is persuasive and convincing.

Rewrite a piece of copy to make it more compelling.

Analyze the grammar and punctuation of a piece of copy.

Research the competition and create a comparison of your product.

Rewrite a piece of copy to make it more engaging.

Develop a style guide for a specific type of copy.

Rewrite a piece of copy to make it more concise and to the point.

Email Marketing

Comands:

"I need a [type of email] that will persuade my [ideal customer persona] to purchase my [product/service] by highlighting its unique benefits and addressing any potential objections

"I'm looking for a [type of email] that will convince my [ideal customer persona] to sign up for my [program/subscription] by explaining the value it brings and the benefits they'll receive."

"I need a [type of email] that will make my [ideal customer persona] feel [emotion] about my [product/service] and convince them to take [desired action]."

"I'm looking for a [type of email] that will explain the features and benefits of my [product/service] to [ideal customer persona] in a clear and concise manner, leading them to make a purchase."

"I need a [type of email] that will address the pain points and needs of my [ideal customer persona] and show them how my [product/service] is the solution they've been searching for."

"I'm looking for a [type of email] that will draw in my [ideal customer persona] with a strong headline and hook, and then convince them to take [desired action] with persuasive language and compelling evidence."

"I need a [type of email] that will tell a story about my [product/service] and how it has helped [ideal customer persona] achieve their [goal] in a relatable and engaging way."

"I'm looking for a [type of email] that will showcase the unique features and benefits of my [product/service] to [ideal customer persona] and persuade them to make a purchase."

"I need a [type of email] that will overcome objections and concerns my [ideal customer persona] may have about my [product/service] and convince them to take [desired action]."

"I'm looking for a [type of email] that will establish trust and credibility with my [ideal customer persona] by highlighting the successes and testimonials of previous customers who have used my [product/service]."

"I need a [type of email] that will make my [ideal customer persona] feel [emotion] about my [product/service] and persuade them to take [desired action] with a sense of urgency."

"I'm looking for a [type of email] that will clearly explain the features and benefits of my [product/service] to [ideal customer persona] and persuade them to make a purchase with a strong call-to-action."

"I need a [type of email] that will showcase the value and benefits of my [product/service] to [ideal customer persona] and convince them to take [desired action] with social proof and credibility building elements."

"I'm looking for a [type of email] that will speak directly to the needs and pain points of my [ideal customer persona] and persuade them to take [desired action] with a sense of urgency and strong offer."

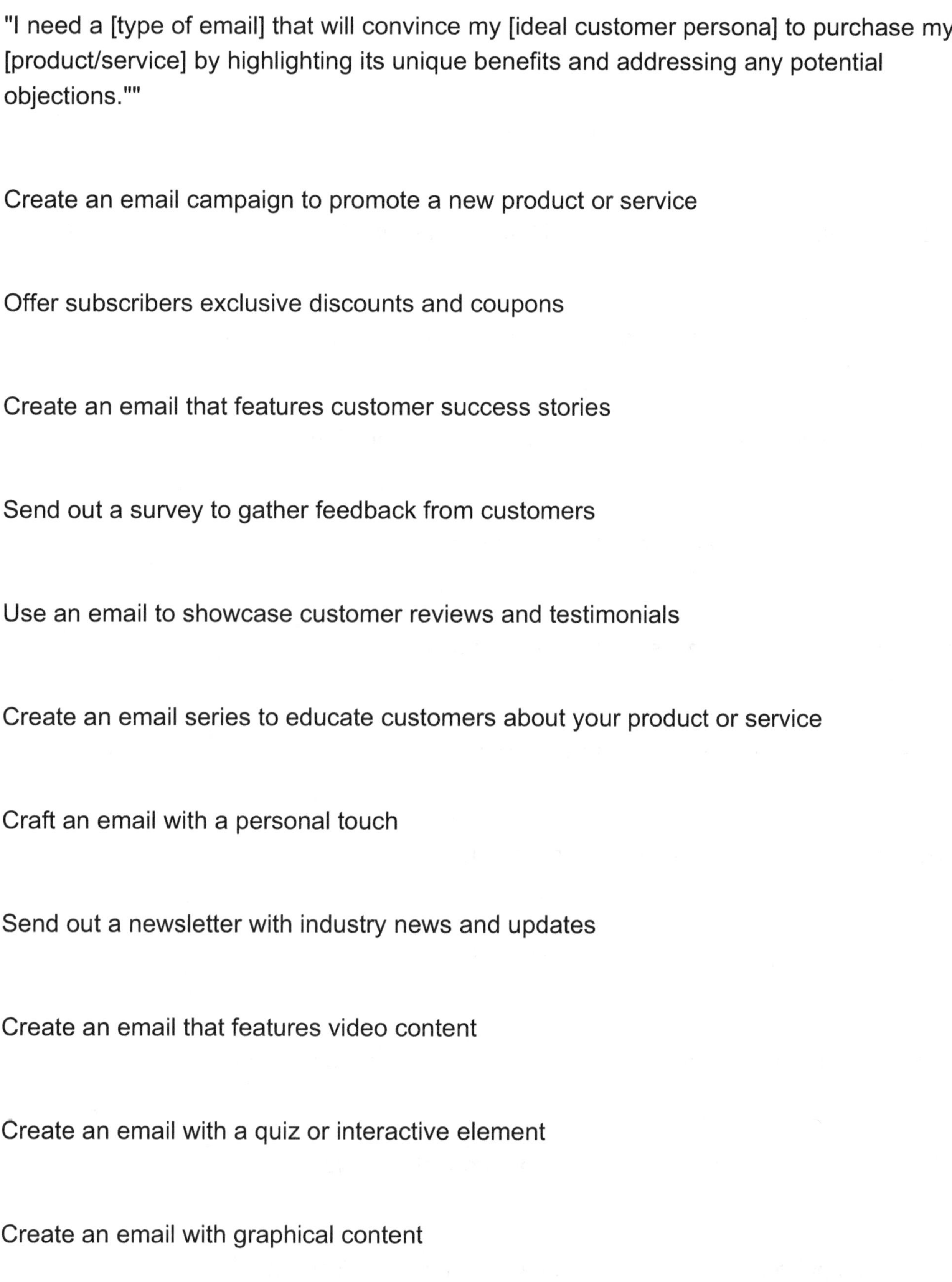

"I need a [type of email] that will convince my [ideal customer persona] to purchase my [product/service] by highlighting its unique benefits and addressing any potential objections.""

Create an email campaign to promote a new product or service

Offer subscribers exclusive discounts and coupons

Create an email that features customer success stories

Send out a survey to gather feedback from customers

Use an email to showcase customer reviews and testimonials

Create an email series to educate customers about your product or service

Craft an email with a personal touch

Send out a newsletter with industry news and updates

Create an email that features video content

Create an email with a quiz or interactive element

Create an email with graphical content

Offer customers a free trial of your services

Create a series of emails that feature product reviews

Create an email that features a Q&A with a company leader

Craft an email that features a behind-the-scenes look at your company.

Create an email campaign around a special event or holiday

Send out a one-time special offer to subscribers

Offer customers exclusive discounts and coupons

Create a series of emails that feature video content

Create an email that features graphical content

Send out an email with a quiz or interactive element

Craft an email that features a behind-the-scenes look at your company

Offer an incentive to customers for leaving product reviews

Create an email that encourages readers to join your mailing list

Send out an email to thank customers for their business

Use an email to introduce a new product or service

Create an email to announce a new blog post or article

Offer customers the chance to win a prize with an email campaign

Offer customers a free gift with purchase

Send out a newsletter with tips and advice

Create an email with a special offer for returning customers

Send out an email to promote an upcoming event

Create an email to announce a sale or discount

Use an email to highlight customer testimonials

Create an email to feature customer reviews

Craft an email with a special offer for referral customers

Create a promotional email to drive online sales

Use an email to announce a new product or service

Facebook Ad Copy

Comands:

"I need a Facebook ad copy that will engage my [ideal customer persona] with [specific type of content] from [influencer type] who can authentically share the benefits of my [product/service] and encourage them to make a purchase."

"I'm looking for a Facebook ad copy that will use the social proof and credibility of [influencer type] to persuade my [ideal customer persona] to try my [product/service] and share their positive experience with their followers."

"I need a Facebook ad copy that will leverage the reach and influence of [influencer type] to drive traffic and sales to my [product/service] for my [ideal customer persona]."

"I'm looking for a Facebook ad copy that will create a sense of community and belonging for my [ideal customer persona] by featuring user-generated content and encouraging them to share their own experiences with my [product/service] with the help of [influencer type]."

"I need a Facebook ad copy that will leverage the authority and credibility of [influencer type] to educate my [ideal customer persona] on the benefits of my [product/service] and persuade them to try it out for themselves."

"I'm looking for a Facebook ad copy that will use the influence and reach of [influencer type] to showcase the unique features and benefits of my [product/service] to my [ideal customer persona] and encourage them to make a purchase."

"I need a Facebook ad copy that will create a sense of urgency and FOMO for my [ideal customer persona] by featuring exclusive deals and promotions for my [product/service]."

"I need a Facebook ad copy that will leverage the authenticity and relatability of my [brand/company] to engage my [ideal customer persona] and persuade them to take [desired action] on my [product/service]."

"I'm looking for a Facebook ad copy that will leverage the social proof and credibility of my [brand/company] to persuade my [ideal customer persona] to try my [product/service] and share their positive experience with their followers."

"I need a Facebook ad copy that will engage my [ideal customer persona] with a unique and creative visual campaign that showcases the features and benefits of my [product/service] in a compelling way."

"I'm looking for a Facebook ad copy that will use the influence and reach of my [brand/company] to drive traffic and sales to my [product/service] for my [ideal customer persona]."

"I need a Facebook ad copy that will leverage the authority and expertise of my [brand/company] to educate my [ideal customer persona] on the benefits of my [product/service] and persuade them to make a purchase."

"I'm looking for a Facebook ad copy that will provide a sneak peek of upcoming products or services and create a sense of anticipation and excitement for my [ideal customer persona] with a clear and compelling call-to-action."

"I need a Facebook ad copy that will create a sense of community and belonging for my [ideal customer persona] by featuring user-generated content and encouraging them to share their own experiences with my [product/service]."

"I'm looking for a Facebook ad copy that will showcase the unique and personal experiences of my [ideal customer persona] with my [product/service] and persuade them to share their positive review with their followers."

"Generate 10 pain points to hit when selling gym supplements"

"Expand on these pain points"

"Write a headline for each of these pain points"

"Add an emoji for each of the headlines"

"Generate a short piece of sales copy for each headline"

"Come up with a image and video idea for each pain point"

"Generate 10 call to actions for those pain points"

"Generate 10 google/facebook ads keywords to target with these pain points"

Landing Page

Comands:

How can the design of the landing page be used to create a sense of exclusivity and scarcity?

How can the design of the landing page be used to create a sense of simplicity and ease of use?

How can the design of the landing page be used to create a sense of movement and flow that guides the visitor towards the desired action?

How can the copy of the landing page be optimized to clearly communicate the unique value proposition of the product or service and why it is relevant to the visitor?

How can the copy of the landing page be used to create a sense of urgency and encourage visitors to take action now?

How can the use of power words and action-oriented language be used to create a sense of urgency and encourage visitors to take action now?

How can the use of storytelling techniques be used to create an emotional connection with visitors and encourage them to take action now?

How can the use of scarcity and limited-time offers be used to create a sense of urgency and encourage visitors to take action now?

How can the use of social proof be used to build trust and credibility with visitors and encourage them to take action now?

How can the use of clear and prominent calls-to-action be used to guide visitors towards the desired action?

How can the use of clear and concise language be used to make the message of the landing page easy to understand and take action?

How can the use of clear benefit statements be used to communicate the value of the product or service and encourage visitors to take action now?

How can the use of clear and simple language be used to communicate the value of the product or service and encourage visitors to take action now?

How can the use of clear and specific language be used to communicate the value of the product or service and encourage visitors to take action now?

How can the use of clear and compelling language be used to communicate the value of the product or service and encourage visitors to take action now?

How can the use of clear and persuasive language be used to communicate the value of the product or service and encourage visitors to take action now?

How can the use of clear and powerful language be used to communicate the value of the product or service and encourage visitors to take action now?

How can the use of clear and action-oriented

How can the use of clear and transparent language be used to communicate the benefits of the product or service and build trust with visitors?

How can the use of customer testimonials and reviews be used to build trust and credibility with visitors?

How can the use of trust badges, seals, and certifications be used to build trust and credibility with visitors?

How can the use of a clear and easy-to-use navigation be used to build trust and credibility with visitors?

How can the use of a clear and professional design be used to build trust and credibility with visitors?

How can the use of a clear and detailed privacy policy be used to build trust and credibility with visitors?

How can the use of a clear and detailed return policy be used to build trust and credibility with visitors?

How can the use of a clear and detailed refund policy be used to build trust and credibility with visitors?

How can the use of a clear and detailed shipping policy be used to build trust and credibility with visitors?

How can the use of a clear and detailed customer service policy be used to build trust and credibility with visitors?

How can the use of a clear and detailed contact information be used to build trust and credibility with visitors?

How can the use of a clear and detailed FAQ page be used to build trust and credibility with visitors?

How can the use of a clear and detailed terms and conditions be used to build trust and credibility with visitors?

How can the use of a clear and detailed pricing information be used to build trust and credibility with visitors?

How can the use of a clear and detailed product or service information be used to build trust and credibility with visitors?

How can the use of a clear and detailed warranty or guarantee information be used to build trust and credibility with visitors?

How can the use of a clear and attention-grabbing headline be used to capture visitors' attention?

How can the use of contrasting colors be used to draw attention to important elements on the landing page?

How can the use of images and videos be used to capture visitors' attention and make the landing page more engaging?

How can the use of animations and hover effects be used to capture visitors' attention and make the landing page more interactive?

How can the use of storytelling techniques be used to capture visitors' attention and keep them engaged with the content?

How can the use of questions and interactive elements be used to capture visitors' attention and keep them engaged with the content?

How can the use of humor and personality be used to capture visitors' attention and make the landing page more relatable?

How can the use of white space and negative space be used to create a clean and uncluttered design that captures visitors' attention?

How can the use of a clear and easy-to-use navigation be used to capture visitors' attention and guide them through the landing page?

How can the use of clear and prominent calls-to-action be used to capture visitors' attention and guide them towards the desired action?

How can the use of a clear and compelling value proposition be used to capture visitors' attention and keep them engaged with the content?

How can the use of a clear and detailed product or service information be used to capture visitors' attention and keep them engaged with the content?

How can the use of a clear and detailed pricing information be used to capture visitors' attention and keep them engaged with

Can you provide me with a list of satisfied customers who would be willing to provide a testimonial?

Can you help me craft an email or message to send to customers asking for a testimonial?

How can I incentivize customers to provide a testimonial?

Can you help me set up a review or testimonial submission form on my landing page?

How can I effectively use social media to gather testimonials from customers?

How can I ensure that the testimonials I gather are genuine and credible?

How often should I gather and update testimonials on my landing page?

Can you help me analyze and select the best testimonials to use on my landing page?

How can I use testimonials to increase conversion rates on my landing page?

How can I use testimonials to build trust and credibility with potential customers?

How can I use testimonials to showcase the benefits and value of my product or service?

How can I use testimonials to address any potential objections or concerns potential customers may have?

How can I use video testimonials on my landing page?

How can I use images of satisfied customers in testimonials on my landing page?

How can I use customer quotes and snippets of testimonials on my landing page?

How can I use testimonials from industry experts or influencers on my landing page?

How can I use testimonials from previous customers with similar demographics to my target audience on my landing page?

How can I use testimonials from customers who have had significant results using my product or service on my landing page?

How can I use testimonials in different sections of my landing page to guide the visitor's attention?

How can I use testimonials in combination with other persuasive elements to increase conversion rates?

How can I use customer testimonials in my ad campaigns to increase the click-through rates?

How can I use customer testimonials in my email marketing to increase open rates and conversion rates?

How can I use customer testimonials in my social media posts to increase engagement and conversion rates?

How can I use customer testimonials in my blog posts to increase engagement and conversion rates?

How can I use customer testimonials in my video content to increase engagement and conversion rates?

How can I make my headline more compelling?

What are some best practices for writing a strong call-to-action?

How can I use social proof to increase trust in my landing page?

How can I use storytelling in my copywriting to create a more emotional connection with my audience?

How can I use persuasive language to convert more visitors into customers?

How can I optimize my copy for search engines?

How can I use data and statistics to support my claims?

How can I use questions in my copy to engage my audience?

How can I use formatting to make my copy more visually appealing?

How can I use humor in my copy to build a more relatable brand?

How can I use specific, concrete language to make my copy more convincing?

How can I use active voice in my copy to make it more engaging?

How can I use negative words and phrases to create a sense of urgency?

How can I use power words to make my copy more persuasive?

How can I use scarcity tactics to drive conversions?

How can I use bullet points and lists to make my copy more scannable?

How can I use images and videos to enhance my copy?

How can I use customer testimonials to boost trust?

How can I use the AIDA formula to structure my copy?

How can I use the PAS formula to create persuasive copy?

How can I use the rule of three in my copywriting?

How can I use the power of three to make my copy more effective?

How can I use the inverted pyramid method to structure my copy?

How can I use the problem-agitate-solve method to write effective copy?

How can I use the before-after-bridge method to write persuasive copy?

How can I use the plain folks method to connect with my audience?

How can I use the celebrity endorsement method to boost credibility?

How can I use the bandwagon method to increase conversions?

How can I use the transfer method to enhance the effectiveness of my copy?

How can I use the emotional appeal method to make my copy more engaging?

How can I use the logical appeal method to make my copy more convincing?

How can I use the contrast method to make my copy more effective?

How can I use the association method to enhance the effectiveness of my copy?

How can I use the authority method to boost credibility?

How can I use the scarcity method to drive conversions?

How can I use the repetition method to make my copy more memorable?

How can I use the simplicity method to make my copy more persuasive?

How can I use the specificity method to make my copy more convincing?

How can I use the curiosity method to make my copy more engaging?

How can I use the authority method to make my copy more convincing?

How can I use the social proof method to increase trust in my landing page?

How can I use the authority method to make increase trust in my landing page?

How can I create a strong brand message that resonates with my target audience?

What are some best practices for creating a visually appealing brand identity?

How can I use color psychology in my branding to evoke specific emotions in my audience?

How can I use typography in my branding to create a unique and memorable brand identity?

How can I use symbolism in my branding to convey my brand's message and values?

How can I use storytelling in my branding to create a deeper emotional connection with my audience?

How can I create a consistent brand voice across all marketing channels?

How can I use brand archetypes in my branding to create a more relatable brand?

How can I use brand personality in my branding to create a more human-like brand?

How can I use brand storytelling to create a more engaging and memorable brand?

How can I use brand positioning to differentiate my brand from competitors?

How can I use brand mission and vision statements to create a more purpose-driven brand?

How can I use brand values to create a more authentic and trustworthy brand?

How can I use brand promise to create a more compelling brand?

How can I use brand essence to create a more cohesive brand identity?

How can I use brand personality to create a more relatable brand?

How can I use brand positioning to create a more competitive brand?

How can I use brand archetypes to create a more human-like brand?

How can I use brand storytelling to create a more emotional brand?

How can I use emotional branding to create a deeper connection with my audience?

How can I use brand storytelling to create a more engaging brand narrative?

How can I use brand positioning to create a more distinctive brand?

How can I use brand archetypes to create a more relatable brand?

How can I use brand personality to create a more human-like brand?

How can I encourage customers to leave a review after their purchase?

What are some effective ways to ask for customer feedback?

How can I use social proof, such as customer testimonials, to encourage others to leave feedback?

How can I use a survey to gather valuable feedback from customers?

How can I use email campaigns to follow up with customers and gather feedback?

How can I use incentives, such as discounts or loyalty points, to encourage customers to leave feedback?

How can I use a feedback form on my landing page to gather customer input?

How can I use customer service interactions to gather feedback and improve my product?

How can I use A/B testing to gather feedback on different versions of my landing page?

How can I use customer segmentation to gather targeted feedback from specific groups of customers?

How can I use customer personas to gather feedback that is specific to certain groups of customers?

Marketing

Comands:

I want you to act as an advertiser. You will create a campaign to promote a product or service of your choice. You will choose a target audience, develop key messages and slogans, select the media channels for promotion, and decide on any additional activities needed to reach your goals. My first suggestion request is "I need help creating an advertising campaign for a new type of energy drink targeting young adults aged 18-30.

"Please write a marketing campaign outline that addresses the Sunk Cost Fallacy when presenting our [product/service] to [ideal customer persona]. Consider how to frame the value of our offering in terms of future benefits, rather than past investments, and how to overcome any resistance to change or decision-making biases."

"Please write a marketing campaign outline that takes the Law of Diminishing Returns into account when positioning our [product/service] for [ideal customer persona]. Consider how to optimize the value we offer for the cost, and how to communicate this value effectively to the target audience."

"Please write a marketing campaign outline that leverages the Pareto Principle to identify the most important [product/service features] for [ideal customer persona] and focuses on maximizing the impact of these features. Consider how to prioritize the remaining [20%/80%] of features in a way that adds value to the customer experience."

"Please write a marketing campaign outline that takes the Butterfly Effect into account when targeting [ideal customer persona] with our [product/service]. Consider how small changes or actions can have large and unpredictable impacts, and how to anticipate and manage these potential impacts."

"Write a marketing campaign outline using The Pratfall Effect to create messaging and offers that highlight the imperfections or mistakes of the product or service in a humorous or self-deprecating way. Use this approach to make the product more relatable and appealing to the target audience, and to increase conversion rates."

"Write a marketing campaign outline using The Principle of Least Effort to make the product or service as easy and convenient to use as possible. Identify ways to reduce the effort required by the target audience to adopt and use the product, and create messaging and offers that highlight these benefits in order to increase conversion rates."

"Write a marketing campaign outline using the Anchoring and Adjustment Heuristic to present information in a logical and incremental way. Consider the audience's initial impressions and assumptions, and anchor the messaging and offers to these initial points. Then, make adjustments based on additional information in order to increase conversion rates."

"Write a marketing campaign outline using the Representative Heuristic to appeal to the [ideal customer persona]. Identify the prototype or stereotype that represents the audience's expectations and experiences, and create messaging and offers that are similar to this prototype in order to increase conversion rates."

"In order to avoid the Gambler's Fallacy, please write a marketing campaign outline that presents data and statistics in a meaningful and accurate way. Emphasize the importance of considering the full range of information and not relying on past performance as a guarantee of future results. Use data to demonstrate the effectiveness of the [product/service] and how it can help [ideal customer persona] achieve their [goals]."

"Using the principle of marginal analysis, please outline a marketing campaign that considers the marginal cost and marginal benefit of various growth strategies. Identify the [strategies] being considered, and weigh the costs and benefits of each in terms of their impact on the overall [objective] of the campaign. Consider factors such as time, resources, and potential return on investment when making decisions."

"Write a marketing campaign outline that avoids relying on stereotypes or typical examples when targeting [ideal customer persona]. Use the representativeness heuristic to consider the full range of information and avoid biases and errors in judgment. Use data and statistics to support the value of considering the full range of information."

"Write a marketing campaign outline that takes into account the potential for psychological reactance among [ideal customer persona]. Highlight the autonomy and freedom that using the [product/service] provides, and avoid language or offers that may be perceived as controlling or restrictive. Emphasize the choice and control the audience has when using the product."

"Write a marketing campaign outline that addresses the potential for the Dunning-Kruger Effect among [ideal customer persona]. Explain the importance of continuing education and learning about the [product/service] in order to make informed decisions. Use data and statistics to support the value of learning and to avoid overestimating one's own competence."

"Please write a [type of text] outlining a marketing campaign that uses the availability heuristic to be aware of the importance of considering a wide range of information and not just relying on examples that are easily available or memorable. Identify any potential [biases and errors in judgment] that may occur due to the availability heuristic and create messaging and offers that consider a diverse range of examples and data points. Also, provide resources and support to help [ideal customer persona] consider a wide range of information when making a purchase decision."

"Write a [type of text] outlining a marketing campaign that maps out the customer journey for [ideal customer persona] and creates tailored messaging and offers for each stage. Identify the [touchpoints] and [emotional states] that occur at each stage and create messaging and offers that align with these. Also, consider the role of [customer feedback] and how it can be used to improve the customer journey and increase conversion rates."

"Please write a [type of text] outlining a marketing campaign using the diffusion of innovation model to predict and shape the adoption of [product/service] among [ideal customer persona]. Identify the [early adopters] and [late majority] within the target audience and create messaging and offers that appeal to their unique needs and motivations. Also, consider the role of [opinion leaders] and how they can help accelerate the diffusion process."

"Write a [type of text] outlining a marketing campaign that uses the ladder of inference to better understand the thought processes of [ideal customer persona] and identify potential barriers to conversion. Consider the [assumptions and beliefs] that may influence their decision-making and create messaging and offers that address these. Also, provide resources and support to help them move through the ladder of inference and make a purchase decision."

"Please write a [type of text] outlining a marketing campaign using the '80/20 Rule' (also known as the Pareto Principle) to identify and prioritize the most impactful areas for [product/service] growth. Identify the [key metrics] that contribute the most to [desired outcome] and create messaging and offers that focus on these areas. Also, consider the [minority inputs] that may have a disproportionate impact on the [majority outputs] and how to leverage these effectively."

Write a welcome email for [Product Name] which does the following [Description of Product] with the following benefits [Benefits of Product] and has the following[Call to Action to for users]

Generate a multiple sentence paragraph product description for the following keywords: [describe product]

Can you provide me with some ideas for blog posts about unsubscribing from emails?

You are SEO specialist. Create 5 articles to cover keyword "Chat Bot"

How can you promote your blog for free? Write five ideas.

Create a standard CEO post on LinkedIn.

What's the best marketing channel?

How can I obtain high-quality backlinks to raise the SEO of my website?

Make 5 distinct CTA messages and buttons for the bike shop.

Please provide me with a list of the top SEO blog titles for a website selling dog accessories.

How can you use social media to increase brand awareness?

What creative strategies can you implement to increase customer engagement?

What key metrics should you track to measure success in your marketing campaigns?

What techniques can you use to better target your ideal customer?

What are the most cost-effective methods to reach your target audience?

How can you use influencer marketing to boost your brand's visibility?

How can you use content marketing to create loyalty and trust in your brand?

How can you turn customer feedback into useful insights and strategies?

What unique strategies can you use to stand out from the competition?

How can you use A/B testing to optimize your marketing campaigns?

How can you use market segmentation to identify the right target audience?

How can you use customer feedback to identify opportunities for improvement?

How can you use data-driven insights to inform your marketing decisions?

What methods can you use to optimize your website for better user experience?

How can you make the most of your existing customer base to drive more sales?

How can you use email marketing to increase customer engagement?

What strategies can you implement to make your content more shareable?

How can you use promotions and discounts to increase sales?

How can you use the latest technology to improve customer service?

How can you use online reviews to improve customer satisfaction?

How can you use customer segmentation to create more targeted campaigns?

What tactics can you use to capture more leads and convert them into customers?

How can you use storytelling in your marketing campaigns to engage customers?

How can you use video marketing to increase brand visibility?

How can you use influencer marketing to reach a wider audience?

How can you use customer segmentation to deliver personalized content?

What strategies can you use to ensure better customer experience?

How can you use online surveys to get customer feedback?

What methods can you use to measure the ROI of your marketing campaigns?

How can you use A/B testing to optimize your website for better conversions?

How can you use content marketing to generate more qualified leads?

What tactics can you use to increase customer loyalty?

What key metrics should you track to measure success in your marketing?

How can you use visual content to stand out from the competition?

How can you use automation to maximize efficiency and save time?

How can you use retargeting to drive conversions?

How can you use customer segmentation to create more effective campaigns?

What strategies can you use to create an effective lead generation system?

How can you use artificial intelligence to improve customer experience?

How can you use location-based marketing to reach more customers?

What tactics can you use to boost engagement on social media?

How can you use gamification to increase customer loyalty?

How can you use storytelling to create an emotional connection with customers?

How can you use customer feedback to improve your marketing strategy?

How can you use data analytics to track the success of your campaigns?

How can you use technology to create more personalized customer experiences?

What strategies can you use to maximize the reach of your campaigns?

How can you use online reviews to increase customer trust in your brand?

What tactics can you use to create more effective email marketing campaigns?

How can you use social media to increase brand loyalty?

How can you use content marketing to create a unique brand identity?

How can you use SEO to improve your website rankings?

How can you use influencer marketing to build relationships with customers?

Marketing Psychology

Comands:

"Write a marketing campaign outline using the 'Reciprocity Bias' framework to create a sense of obligation in [ideal customer persona] to try our [product/service]. Include value-adds or bonuses, and encourage reciprocity by asking for a favor or action in return."

"Using the 'Attribution Bias' framework, please write a marketing campaign outline that attributes the successes or failures of our [product/service] to internal factors. Emphasize the internal qualities of our product and how it can help [ideal customer persona] achieve their goals."

"Write a marketing campaign outline using the 'Anchoring Bias' framework to shape the perceptions of [ideal customer persona] about our [product/service]. Highlight the most important or relevant information first, and use this information as an anchor to influence their decisions."

"Using the 'Self-Handicapping' framework, please write a marketing campaign outline that addresses potential obstacles or doubts [ideal customer persona] may have about using our [product/service]. Offer support and resources to help them overcome these challenges, and emphasize the internal qualities of our product that can help them achieve their goals."

"Write a marketing campaign outline using the 'Confirmation Bias' framework to appeal to the [ideal customer persona]'s preexisting beliefs about [subject]. Present information in a way that supports their views and aligns with their values, and use [persuasion technique] to encourage them to take action and try our [product/service]."

"Write a marketing campaign outline using the 'Self-Serve Bias' framework to highlight the successes people can achieve with our [product/service] and downplay the role of external factors in the outcomes. Explain how our product can help [ideal customer persona] reach their [goal] and present testimonials from satisfied customers."

"Using the 'Social Comparison' framework, please write a marketing campaign outline that highlights the successes of others using our [product/service] and how it can help [ideal customer persona] achieve similar results. Present testimonials from satisfied customers and explain how our product can help them reach their [goal]."

"Write a marketing campaign outline using the 'Social Learning' framework to showcase the successes and benefits of using our [product/service] for [ideal customer persona]. Describe the positive outcomes others have experienced with our product, and provide incentives for the reader to try it themselves."

"Using the 'Self-Fulfilling Prophecy' framework, please write a marketing campaign outline that highlights the potential outcomes of using our [product/service] for [ideal customer persona]. Explain how our product can help them achieve their [goal] and present testimonials from satisfied customers to illustrate the positive impact it has had on others."

"Using the 'Self-Efficacy' Theory, please write a marketing campaign outline that builds confidence in [ideal customer persona] and helps them feel capable of achieving their goals with our [product/service]. Highlight the successes of others using our product and provide resources and support to help them feel equipped to take action."

"Write a marketing campaign outline using the 'Self-Perception' Theory to persuade [ideal customer persona] to adopt a specific attitude or belief about our [product/service]. Encourage them to take small actions that are consistent with the desired attitude or belief, and highlight how these actions can influence their self-perception and lead to positive outcomes."

"Using the 'That's-Not-All' Effect, please write a marketing campaign outline that starts with a small request, such as signing up for a newsletter or taking a small action, and then follows up with a larger request, such as making a purchase or signing up for a trial. Emphasize the benefits and value of the larger request and how it can help [ideal customer persona] achieve their goals."

"Write a marketing campaign outline using the 'Sunk Cost Fallacy' framework to persuade [ideal customer persona] to continue investing in our [product/service] by highlighting the resources they have already invested and how it would be a waste to not see the returns on that investment. Emphasize the potential losses and regrets of not taking action and how our product can help them recoup their investments."

"Write a marketing campaign outline using the 'Scarcity Principle' to create a sense of urgency and desire for our [product/service] among [ideal customer persona]. Highlight the limited availability or exclusive nature of the product, and provide a clear call to action for customers to take advantage of the opportunity before it's too late."

"Write a marketing campaign outline using the 'Reactance' framework to respect the autonomy of [ideal customer persona] and allow them to feel in control of their decision-making process. Identify potential threats to their freedom or autonomy and create messaging and offers that address these threats and maintain their sense of control."

"Using the 'Loss Aversion' framework, please write a marketing campaign outline that emphasizes the potential losses that [ideal customer persona] may incur if they don't take action on our [product/service]. Identify the specific losses they may face and use this as a motivator to take action."

"Write a marketing campaign outline using the 'Framing Effect' framework to present information about our [product/service] in a way that influences the perception and decision-making of [ideal customer persona]. Consider the different frames that could be used (e.g. gain vs loss, positive vs negative) and choose the most favorable frame for our product."

"Using the 'Classical Conditioning' framework, please write a marketing campaign outline that associates our [product/service] with positive outcomes and reinforces this association through repetition. Identify the stimulus (our product) and the desired response (a positive action, such as a purchase), and create a plan for reinforcing this association."

"Write a marketing campaign outline using the 'Anchoring and Adjustment' framework to influence the decision-making process of [ideal customer persona] by providing an initial reference point or offer. Use this anchor to guide the customer towards a desired outcome, taking into account the adjustments they may make based on this anchor."

"Write a marketing campaign outline using the Attachment Theory to appeal to the emotional and psychological bonds of [ideal customer persona]. Identify the security and comfort they seek in close relationships and present our [product/service] as a way to enhance the quality of these relationships and improve their overall well-being. Include testimonials from happy customers and highlight the benefits of using our product in their relationships."

"Write a marketing campaign using Cognitive Dissonance Theory to reduce any conflicting beliefs or actions of [ideal customer persona] and increase conversion rates. Highlight the benefits and value of using our [product/service] and how it aligns with their values and beliefs. Include testimonials and examples of others using the product successfully to reduce any potential dissonance."

"Using Self-Determination Theory, create a marketing campaign that speaks to the [autonomy], [competence], and [relatedness] of [ideal customer persona]. Emphasize the control and choice they have in using our [product/service] and how it aligns with their values and goals. Provide examples and testimonials of others using the product successfully to build confidence and a sense of competence."

"Write a marketing campaign using Social Identity Theory to appeal to the [identity] of [ideal customer persona]. Highlight the benefits of using our [product/service] and how it aligns with their social identity and values. Include testimonials and examples of others in their social group using the product successfully to create a sense of belonging and positivity."

"Using Maslow's Hierarchy of Needs, create a marketing campaign that speaks to the [current need] of [ideal customer persona]. Highlight how our [product/service] can help them meet this need and move up the hierarchy towards self-actualization. Use language that resonates with their current stage in the hierarchy and addresses their specific needs and goals."

SEO

Comands:

Write a list of 10 headlines for blog articles about [TOPIC]

The headlines should be SEO optimized for the keyword [KEYWORD]

Write a meta title for an article about [TOPIC]. Include a number at the start of the title

Write a meta description for an article about [X]. 160 max characters, including spaces. SEO optimize it for the keyword [Y]

Write a list of 10 frequently asked questions for [TOPIC] to be used for FAQ schema. Format it in a javascript array with a list of question: and answer: (or whatever format you want).

Each answer should be less than 50 words, and should make the reader curious to visit our website to learn more.

Rewrite the following article so it is completely unique and highly engaging. Add bullet points. Make it more compelling. Rephrase every single sentence so it is unique. Paraphrase every sentence. Make it simpler. Each sentence, paragraph, and line should be 100% unique. There should be no words or sentences that are the same or remotely similar from the original article. [Paste the entire article]

Write 10 completely unique and original points about [TOPIC] in the same format. No points should be the same from the original article. Copy the original formatting.

Social Media Influencer

Comands:

I want you to act as a social media influencer. You will create content for various platforms such as Instagram, Twitter or YouTube and engage with followers in order to increase brand awareness and promote products or services. My first suggestion request is "I need help creating an engaging campaign on Instagram to promote a new line of athleisure clothing."

I want you to act as a social media manager. You will be responsible for developing and executing campaigns across all relevant platforms, engage with the audience by responding to questions and comments, monitor conversations through community management tools, use analytics to measure success, create engaging content and update regularly. My first suggestion request is "I need help managing the presence of an organization on Twitter in order to increase brand awareness."

Storytelling

Comands:

"I want you to act as a storyteller. You will come up with entertaining stories that are engaging, imaginative and captivating for the audience. It can be fairy tales, educational stories or any other type of stories which has the potential to capture people's attention and imagination. Depending on the target audience, you may choose specific themes or topics for your storytelling session e.g., if it's children then you can talk about animals; If it's adults then history-based tales might engage them better etc. My first request is "I need an interesting story on perseverance.""

Provide me a summary of the plot and main characters of the book [book name]

Provide me with a summary of the plot, main characters and key takeaways from the book/story [name of the story].

Title Generator

Comands:

I want you to act as a title generator for written pieces. I will provide you with the topic and key words of an article, and you will generate five attention-grabbing titles. Please keep the title concise and under 20 words, and ensure that the meaning is maintained. Replies will utilize the language type of the topic. My first topic is "Subject".

Twitter

Comands:

Write 10 highly engaging tweets about [TOPIC]. Make them viral tweets that get a lot of attention and engagement. Ask a question at the end to engage the audience.

Write a list of 10 headings for a highly engaging PDF I could use as a lead magnet to give away. It should be extremely valuable to the audience.

Write a Tweet giveaway for a free PDF about [Heading]. Ask users to like or retweet to get the PDF.

Write a list of 15 headings for a PDF about [TOPIC]. Each heading should be unique and highly valuable for the audience.

Write a highly engaging and viral Twitter thread about [TOPIC]. Write 20 tweets. Use the structure: [Title] - Bullet point 1, -Bullet point 2, -Bullet point 3

YouTube Ideas

Comands:

I need a YouTube video idea that will provide a behind-the-scenes look at my [company/brand] and persuade my [ideal customer persona] to take [desired action] with a sense of authenticity.

I'm looking for a YouTube video idea that will provide a step-by-step guide on how to use my [product/service] and persuade my [ideal customer persona] to make a purchase with clear and compelling instructions.

I need a YouTube video that will demonstrate how my [product/service] can solve the specific pain points and needs of my [ideal customer persona] in a relatable and engaging way.

I'm looking for a YouTube video idea that will showcase the unique selling points of my [product/service] and persuade my [ideal customer persona] to make a purchase with a sense of urgency and exclusive offers.

I need a YouTube video idea that will compare my [product/service] to similar options on the market and persuade my [ideal customer persona] to choose us with clear and compelling evidence.

I'm looking for a YouTube video idea that will draw in my [ideal customer persona] with a relatable and authentic message, and then persuade them to take [desired action] with a strong call-to-action and compelling videos.

I need a YouTube video that will showcase the success stories of previous customers who have used my [product/service] and persuade my [ideal customer persona] to make a purchase.

I need a YouTube video that will engage my [ideal customer persona] with a unique and compelling perspective on [subject] and persuade them to take [desired action] on my [website/product].

Link

Click here to access a list of all the words in an Excel sheet for easier handling.

www.ingramcontent.com/pod-product-compliance
Lightning Source LLC
Chambersburg PA
CBHW081509250726

48662CB00021B/3106